MOOOI480UM.

Adventures
IN SPACE

KT-446-906

A Mother's

This book is to be returned on or before the last date
stamped below.

Learning Services
City of Westminster College

Maida Vale Centre
London W9 2NR
020 7258 2849

For my girls Katie, Ellie and Lydia

Performance Rights

All rights whatsoever in these plays are strictly reserved, and professional and amateur applications for permission to perform them, etc., must be made in advance before rehearsals begin, to: Lucy Johnson, Hodder and Stoughton Educational, English and Drama Department, 338 Euston Road, London NW1 3BH.

Orders: please contact Bookpoint Ltd, 39 Milton Park, Abingdon, Oxon OX14 4TD. Telephone: (44) 01235 400454, Fax: (44) 01235 400454. Lines are open from 9.00 – 6.00, Monday to Saturday, with a 24 hour message answering service. Email address: orders@bookpoint.co.uk

British Library Cataloguing in Publication Data
A catalogue record for this title is available from The British Library

ISBN 0 340 77685 4

First published 2000
Impression number   10 9 8 7 6 5 4 3 2 1
Year   2006 2005 2004 2003 2002 2001 2000

Cover photograph © Hulton Getty
Typeset by Fakenham Photosetting Limited, Fakenham, Norfolk.
Printed in Great Britain for Hodder & Stoughton Educational, a division of Hodder Headline Plc, 338 Euston Road, London NW1 3BH by Redwood Books, Trowbridge, Wiltshire.

CONTENTS

Introduction iv
List of Characters v

1. The Ghosts 1
2. Absence and Loss 4
3. Darkness 11
4. The Factory 13
5. The Picnic in the Hills 18
6. Baptista and Ernesto 22
7. The Fishwives 25
8. The Festival 29
9. The River of Death 35
10. The Mother 38
11. A Death 40
12. The News 41
13. The Search/The Prison 46
14. The Fight goes on 50
15. They Dance Alone 51

Performance Materials 53
Performance Exercises 55
Performance Notes and Exercises 60
Context Notes for the Performer 71
An Author's Note 77

INTRODUCTION

A Mother's Voice is ideally suited to student companies, senior pupils within schools and other companies looking for challenging material for a predominantly female group of performers. There is a need for a minimum of 2–3 male roles. In the original production the central roles of the Father and Ernesto were played by the same actor. The shadows (gunmen) should be played by males and the officials may be of either gender.

The production is set in a 'mythical' Central/South American country and this is reflected in the music and costume. Human rights abuses and cases of 'disappearance' are not limited to any particular nation or country. The dialogue is largely universal in quality and with some subtle changes of names and music there is no reason why it can not be set against the background of your choice.

A Mother's Voice allows for:

1. a variable size cast with the possibility of multiple role playing by all but those playing the central characters
2. through the use of multiple roles, the ability to create balanced roles for all performers
3. the undertaking of considerable research into the roles and situations depicted
4. flexibility in the realisation of areas of the script with responsibility given to individual performers
5. exciting and risk taking physical theatre and the inclusion of elements of dance
6. an ensemble performance and the creation of a strong group identity.

Performance Exercises and **Context Notes for the Performer** are included at the back of the text to kick-start the performance project.

LIST OF CHARACTERS

The Family:
Constantina, Baptista, Francisca, Isabel, Maria

The Land of the Dead:
The Ghosts (3)
The Voices of the Dead
The Dream Mother
The Father

The Factory:
Ernesto
The Factory Girls (6)

The Village:
Catalina, Juanita, Dolores, Carmen (Fishwives)
The Gossips (10)
Dancers and the Festival Crowd
The Body of the Father

The State:
The Shadows (2)
The Officials (2)

The Ghosts

Music plays. The ghosts enter the space as if being chased — or are they doing the chasing? They pause to gain their breath. In the space they seem alarmed and wary. They look around as if claiming the space as their own and intimidating any onlookers. After some moments they speak

Ghost 1   Whispers . . .

Ghost 2   . . . whispers all around. . .

Ghost 3   . . . whispers that cry to be heard . . .

Ghost 1   . . . whispers that shout and scream and pound and tear.

Ghost 2   Let me in.

Ghost 3   Let me in.

Ghost 1   And plead.

Ghost 2   Let me in.

Ghost 1   But she won't . . .

Ghost 2   . . . won't let them in.

Ghost 3   Her world, too fragile . . .

Ghost 1   . . . too vulnerable . . .

Ghost 3   . . . to withstand the. . .

All   SHOCK

Ghost 1   Keep them out.

Ghost 2   Yes keep them out.

Ghost 1   For now.

Ghost 3	But she will always . . .
Ghost 2	. . . always . . .
Ghost 1	. . . know they are there.
Ghost 2	Scratching . . .
Ghost 3	. . . gnawing . . .
Ghost 2	. . . rasping . . .
Ghost 1	. . . at the corners of her life.
Ghost 2	And one day . . .
Ghost 3	. . . yes one day . . .
Ghost 1	. . . they will force their way in.
Ghost 2	Squeezing through the shutters.
Ghost 3	Squirming under the doors.
Ghost 1	Writhing through the cracks in the walls.
Ghost 3	. . . then she will see . . .
Ghost 2	. . . then she will know . . .
Ghost 1	. . . and her life will be filled with a dark, dark light.

The 'dead' enter slowly, whispering. Their whispers are the nagging doubts and fears in the Mother's mind. They take up positions in the space. The Dream Mother enters at one end of the arena space and stops. The dead see her, there is a moment of silence. The dead then form into two lines presenting a corridor for the Dream Mother – the 'procession of whispers'. She slowly walks between them and as she passes each one so the whispers begin again. Once through the dead she stops and their lines break and they form positions around her. The voices are the dead

Voice	Why are you here Constantia?

Voice	Why do you dwell in the land of the dead?
D. Mother	I am not in the land of the dead.
Voice	We are the dead.

With agonised cries they form postures of death and freeze in them

Voice	Why do you call to us?
D. Mother	I call to him.

The father enters the space and stands in front of her. He moves like one of the dead

Voice	But he is one of us.
D. Mother	No.
Voice	He **is** one of us.
D. Mother	No. I will not listen to you. Get out of my dreams. You don't belong here. I don't want you here. The whispers mean nothing. I'll not listen.
Father	(flatly) Constantia.
D. Mother	Ramon. My sweet Ramon.
Father	Constantia.

They embrace. The father barely reacts

D. Mother	Ramon. When are you coming home? Come home soon Ramon. I miss you so much.
Voice	The truth Constantia . . .
Voice	. . . listen to the truth.
D. Mother	It's all lies. I will not listen to lies.
Father	Constantia.

D. Mother   Ramon, come home soon. I'm waiting for you.
                       I love you Ramon. Whatever it is I will forgive
                       you. Whatever I have done, I will put it right.
                       Just come home soon.

Voices   Mother, Mother, Mother (*repeats as the dead close on
                       the father*).

*The dead slowly surround the father cutting him off from the Dream Mother. She
stays rooted to the spot but grows more fearful as they close on him, taking him
from her. She reaches out to him*

D. Mother   No. (*more firmly*) No!

Baptista   (*Off stage*) Mother! Mother! Mother, what is
                       wrong?

·2·

Absence and Loss

*The lights fade and come up on Constantia who is standing by the table lost in
her thoughts mirroring the final stance of the Dream Mother. She is mouthing
the word 'No'. In the blackout the dead exit, but the ghosts gather in a position
where they can silently observe the scene that follows*

Baptista   (*Approaching and putting a hand on her shoulder*)
                       Mother.

Constantia   (*Startled out of her dream*) What?

Baptista   Is anything the matter?

Constantia   No of course not. I was just lost in my
                       thoughts. It is strange, but in my dreams I am
                       always young again. My hair is long and

flowing and my bones do not ache. My skin is still smooth and fresh, not lined and parched as it is now. I feel full of life and hope. I was thought to be quite a beauty when I was young, Baptista.

Baptista   You are still beautiful Mardre.

Constantia   (*Laughs becoming herself again*) Well now that you are home we should prepare the table. Isabel and Maria are in the kitchen.

They begin to lay cutlery and plates on the table

Baptista   (*Calling*) Isabel! Maria! Hurry up. I'm starving.

Constantia   Baptista please. Have I brought you up to caterwaul like some fishwife. A good man does not want a wife that shrieks so!

Baptista   I am calling for my supper Mother, not a husband.

Constantia   It is just as well. Mixing with those factory girls is having a bad influence on you.

Baptista   The girls are fine. They are good girls – well most of them. It is the life in the factory that makes them less refined.

Constantia   I still do not like you working there.

Baptista   What else can I do?

Constantia   Find a man.

Francisca   (*Entering*) Like I did you mean!

Constantia   Francisca! This is a surprise. Yes like you. You should be like your big sister here. If she found a man then so can you.

Francisca	Well, I found Basilio. I'm not certain I found a man.
Constantia	Still not pregnant then?
Francisca	Mother. What a thing to ask the moment I step through the door.
Constantia	Well?
Francisca	No, I'm not pregnant.
Constantia	Then it's about time you were. I want to be a grandmother soon. Is everything all right between you? There is a woman in the village who has potions you know.
Francisca	Mother! Basilio is fine. I thought I would come visiting.
Constantia	And you are very welcome. We will lay an extra place for supper.

They embrace in greeting. Isabel and Maria enter with bread, cheese and bowls of fruit

Baptista	About time.
Isabel	The supper is almost ready Mother. Will you come and look? I think, I have done everything right.
Constantia	I am sure you have but I will come to make certain. I think I can smell something burning.
Isabel	Oh no.

Isabel and Constantia exit. The others watch them go

Francisca	How has she been?

Maria	Much the same. Perhaps a little worse.
Francisca	Does she talk about him?
Maria	As if he has just stepped out of the door and will be back at any moment.
Francisca	Where does she think he is?
Baptista	She does not seem to consider that important. She only plans for when he comes back.
Maria	She does not even seem curious.
Francisca	This cannot go on. She must see reason.
Maria	There is no reason here any more. She seems almost cheerful sometimes, as if she must keep us all happy while he is away. And it is so hard, Francisca. You do not know what it is like. My heart is breaking. All the time, inside, I feel . . . tight like I am about to burst. Padre is dead, Francisca, I know it. Yet I cannot speak of it. And more than anything in the world I want father to come back; to feel his strong arms around me; to comfort me; to say 'Maria – little one – it will be all right'.

Overwhelmed and weeping, Maria throws herself on Francisca. Francisca and Baptista look at each other

Francisca	There, there Maria. It is hard. It is hard on all of us.
Maria	(*Recovering*) But they have not found a body, perhaps . . .
Francisca	No, Maria – do not start to even dream it. In the village they say for certain, it was the police that took him.

Baptista	(*Confessing*) I have been to them again.
Francisca	Baptista – no more. We want no more grief. Promise you will go no more.
Baptista	I promise, Francisca.
Francisca	It has been more than two months now. If he was being held prisoner, we would have been told by now. They would want us to suffer the agony of knowing where he was.
Baptista	Without his body I do not think Mother will ever admit that he is dead.
Francisca	(*She ponders the point then resolves herself*) This has to stop. She has to stop punishing us all like this. Baptista, do not lay Padre's place tonight.
Maria	But Francisca, Mother will . . .
Baptista	She is right, Maria. We must face this. (*She moves her father's setting to Francisca's place.*)
Francisca	I will talk to her.

They finish moving the things and then gather together, waiting for their Mother to return. The ghosts speak up

Ghost 3	His place. His chair.
Ghost 2	A space that defines his absence . . .
Ghost 1	. . . a space that defines their loss . . .
Ghost 3	. . . where once there was a father and husband . . .
Ghost 1	. . . now there is just a chair.

Isabel and Constantia return with the food

Constantia	Here we are at last.

Isabel	We were just in time. It had started to stick to the bottom of the pot but I rescued it. With some help from Mother.
Constantia	She is too modest. I helped only a little. My Isabel is an excellent cook.
Isabel	I made it from one of Madre's recipes so it is bound to be good!
Constantia	Come along, all of you. Stop dithering. There is eating to be done. *(She notices there is no place setting for the father)* Oh dear, all of you girls are in a forgetful mood tonight. Isabel, we are one short. Go and fetch another place setting.
Francisca	No Isabel. Do not go. There is no need.
Isabel	But Mother said . . .
Constantia	We need one more, Isabel.
Francisca	Mother, there are five of us here. We need only five places.
Isabel	But what about Father?
Constantia	Well Francisca?
Francisca	He does not need a place.
Constantia	And if your father comes through that door tonight, what will he think when he sees us with no place set for him!
Francisca	Mother, he will not come through that door. He will never come through that door.
Isabel	Why do you say he will never come through the door? Of course he will.
Constantia	Ignore her, Isabel. She is being foolish.

Francisca	Mother, this must stop for all our sakes.
Constantia	What must stop, Francisca?
Francisca	Father is dead. He is not coming back.

There is a moment, seemingly frozen in time

Isabel	Is Father dead, Mother? Is he?
Constantia	No he is not. Now I will have no more of this. Isabel fetch the place setting at once.

Isabel exits

Baptista	Mother, please you must . . .
Constantia	No more. I know that this is a difficult time. But Isabel is younger than all of you and yet she retains her faith. Do you not think I would know if your father was dead? I would know it here *(she indicates her heart)*.
Francisca	Then where is he Madre? He would not desert us. Where do you think he has gone?
Constantia	Wherever he is, he will have his reasons. We must place our trust in God and look to his return.
Baptista	But in the village they say . . .
Constantia	Only a fool listens to what they say. They gossip and lie.
Francisca	Then, how long are we going to wait Mother? How long?
Constantia	How long do you think your Father would wait for you to return Francisca?

A long heavy awkward silence during which Isabel returns

Constantia	Very well. Now no more such talk. Lay your father's place Isabel.
Isabel	Yes Mother.

She does so and they take their seats. They settle to prayer

Constantia	Dear God. As we settle to this meal we pray for Ramon, a good husband and father. Tend to him and comfort him. Hasten his return and give my children the strength and faith to sustain them in his absence.

As they open their eyes they look at the space occupied by the chair

Constantia	Now, let us eat.

Pause. A frozen moment then the children exit. The mother looks up

·3·

Darkness

Constantia	I know you are there Ramon. I will wait for eternity for your return. When I close my eyes I can . . .

Scene switches to the Dream Mother and the Father in an embrace. The Father is more human in this scene

D. Mother	. . . feel the warmth of your embrace and the touch of your lips on mine. Look into the depths of your eyes and feel the strength in your arms. When you hold me Ramon, I want to never let you go.
Father	(*Retreating*) But you must Constantia, you must

let me go. I cannot bear to see you in such pain. And your pain is my pain. Your despair is my anguish.

D. Mother Where are you going Ramon? Come back to me. Come back to us. We need you Ramon.

Father I have another path to tread now Constantia. A path I must tread alone.

D. Mother No stay here. Stay with me.

Father I am in agony Constantia.

D. Mother Then let me hold you, tend to you, love and comfort you.

The Ghosts who have been watching all this time begin to softly whisper 'Ramon'

Father It cannot be Constantia. They are calling to me. I must go.

The light begins to fade on the Father as he slowly moves towards the ghosts and exits

D. Mother I will have faith Ramon. I will not listen to their whispers. Come to me soon Ramon. Do not slip into their . . .

We switch back to the real mother

Constantia . . . darkness.

She sits for a moment and seems to feel all the tiredness in the world. Then she gathers herself. Lights a candle and exits with it. The ghosts approach the table

Ghost 3 Yes, mother. Keep the dark at bay

Ghost 2 For as long as you can.

Ghost 1 But when your last candle flickers out . . .

Ghost 3 . . . and all hope is gone.

Ghost 2	There will be only blackness.

The ghosts depart.

·4·

The Factory

A whistle blows. The sound of voices is heard then the factory workers enter. They talk together and seem tired but grateful for the opportunity to meet on their break. They settle to their food then Ernesto enters and immediately is the centre of the girls' attention

Girl 1	Hey Ernesto, there is still no guard on my machine. I thought you said you were going to see the bosses about it.
Ernesto	I have seen them. They promised me they would have one fitted soon.
Girl 2	Promises, promises! All we ever get is promises Ernesto.
Girl 3	Yes, we've heard it all before. When is something going to be done?
Girl 1	You are supposed to be our representative Ernesto. We want something done.
Girl 4	Look at my sleeve Ernesto. It got caught again this morning. I do not want to be like Anita Ramirez and have a stump where my hand should be.
Ernesto	Then until the guards are fitted, roll your sleeves up.

There is a generally negative reaction

Girl 2	Roll up your sleeves Ernesto. Is that the best you can do? Have you forgotten about Margarita? When her hair got caught! Now her children have no mother. Have you forgotten the sight we saw?
Ernesto	Of course not. But I can only do what I can do.
Girl 5	And what can you do Ernesto? You can come and do something for me if you like!
Girl 6	How is your machinery Ernesto? All in working order I hope.

General laughter

Ernesto	Please ladies.
Girl 3	Did you say 'Please' Ernesto – girls look, he's asking for it!
Ernesto	This is serious. All I can do is talk to the bosses. I do talk to them but I cannot force them to listen. Only you can do that.
Girl 2	How Ernesto?
Ernesto	They will not bother to fit guards to the machines when they know that to fit a guard to one machine will cost twice as much as it does to employ one of you. They would prefer to wait until you are injured and then replace you. It's cheaper.

General agreement

Ernesto	They do not care about you or me. They care about only money. If you want them to listen then you must take action.

Girl 1	Like what Ernesto?
Ernesto	Perhaps a walk out, or down tools or even a strike.

This gets a derisory response

Girl 2	Ernesto, what is the point of striking? They would just sack us and replace us with new workers.
Girl 1	You are an idealist Ernesto. We have children to feed.
Girl 5	They protested at my husband's factory about conditions. The police drove straight through them. The next day they were back at work – except for the four who are dead.
Baptista	Then what is Ernesto to do? How can he do anything if we do not help!
Girl 4	Are you suggesting a strike Baptista?
Baptista	Perhaps.
Girl 5	Stop trying to impress Ernesto, Baptista.
Girl 6	He is impressed enough already.
Baptista	What about a protest then – or a petition? If we all sign a petition then they might listen.
Girl 3	What's the point. They'll just ignore it.
Ernesto	We could at least try. Shall I draw up a petition?

There is a neutral and uncommitted response

Baptista	I will sign it.

Girl 3   You have to be careful what you put your name to around here, Baptista.

Others around agree with this statement

Girl 2   Just keep nagging them for us Ernesto.

Girl 4   Yes. Keep it up Ernesto!

There are cat calls and remarks. Ernesto shrugs as if giving up. Baptista sits down watched by Ernesto who decides to approach her. This is closely watched by the others.

Ernesto   It is a hard job to get them to really **do** anything, Baptista. But I understand. There is much to fear.

Baptista   Then nothing will ever change.

Ernesto   You want to bring about change, Baptista?

Baptista   There are too many things wrong in our country Ernesto. Too much fear and too much cruelty. There is ... was, this boy. A street boy. When I got off the bus in the mornings he would be there, playing his flute, begging for money. He had a cheeky grin and a lovely face. Eleven years old, Ernesto and abandoned on the streets. I always gave him something – some food at least. He called me 'his beautiful Seniorita'. I never knew his name ...

One day, when I got off the bus, he was not there. I asked one of the others and they said that a van full of men had come in the night and taken him away. Three days later he was there again. But his smile was gone.

A rich man in the city. His child had problems with his sight and needed an operation. So

they had taken his eyes Ernesto. My little flute
player was blind. He had lost his flute. He
knew my voice when I spoke to him. I gave
him all my food.

Two weeks later he was gone again. I have not
seen him since.

Ernesto   Baptista, if you are serious about wanting
change ...

Baptista   I am.

Ernesto   Well, there is a meeting – a political meeting –
tomorrow night. Would you like to come?

Baptista   I do not know ...

Ernesto   There would be others there. You would not be
on your own.

Baptista   (*She pauses for a moment*) ... yes, I would like to
go Ernesto.

Ernesto   Shall I meet you outside the factory gates then
– to take you – at about 8 o'clock?

Baptista   That would be fine.

Ernesto   I look forward to it.

Ernesto rises and moves away. The others quickly swoop on Baptista

Girl 5   What did he say Baptista?

Girl 6   Did he ask you out?

Baptista   Well, in a way. I am seeing him tomorrow
night.

Big reaction from the girls

Girl 4   Where is he taking you Baptista?

Baptista	To a meeting.
Girl 6	A meeting?
Baptista	A political meeting.

There is a mocking response from the girls

Girl 5	Just don't let him show you his manifesto on your first date!

There is much laughter. The whistle goes again and the girls all go back into the 'factory'.

·5·

The Picnic in the Hills

Constantia enters. She is holding a photograph of her husband. She places it on the table and sits looking at it

Constantia	Where are you Ramon? The girls think that you are not coming back Ramon. I know that you will.
	Your Baptista has gone out tonight. She says that it is with girls from her factory – there was something in the way she said it that makes me think there is a boy. You should be here to watch over her Ramon. To see that she is sensible. You know how headstrong she is.
	Soon it will be the Festival again in Huanos in the hills. I think that there, we were the happiest of all. When the girls were younger – and we were younger. They were good times Ramon. The best times.

She closes her eyes and we go into her dream. The dream is full of life and happiness. The father is as he was in real life

Maria   (Off stage) Father, Father catch me!

Father   (Off stage) I am coming for you Maria.

Maria enters running, chased by her father. The others follow closely behind. Isabel holding the Dream Mother's hand. The father catches Maria and sweeps her off her feet

Father   Got you little one.

D. Mother   Not so little now Ramon.

Father   She will always be my little one Constantia. Will you not Maria!

He puts her down and tickles her

Maria   Let me go. Let me go!

Francisca   You are a monster Padre!

Father   A monster is it.

He pulls a monster face and chases after them all. There are shrieks and screams. He catches hold of the Dream Mother and picks her up in his arms

Father   I will carry you to my castle sweet damsel.

D. Mother   Sweet Damsel! Put me down Ramon.

Father   Just one kiss.

D. Mother   Ramon!

Father   Is it so scandalous that a husband should wish to kiss his beautiful wife?

Baptista   Give in Mother. You know what Padre is like.

Isabel   Yes and I am starving.

D. Mother   Very well.

They kiss

D. Mother   Now enough of this nonsense. Will this be good enough for our picnic?

Father   The sun is shining, the hills are beautiful and I am surrounded by my wonderful family. What could be better!

Francisca   We can look down on the village from up here. Doesn't it look wonderful. All of the flags and the colours.

Isabel   We will see the procession won't we Mother?

Distant music from the village begins to play

D. Mother   Of course Isabel. It is not until later on. But first we eat.

Baptista   I can hear music.

Maria   It is from the bands in the village.

Father   Music Mother!

He sidles up to the Dream Mother and despite her reserve they begin to dance. The others look on and clap and cheer. With a swirl they break apart

D. Mother   What has got into you today Ramon!

Father   Life Constantia. Can you not feel it! It is good to be alive on a day like this.

Maria   Another game Father!

D. Mother   Maria, we will never eat!

Maria   It will build up our appetites Madre. Please.

Father   What will it be?

Baptista   Catch.

Isabel   Who will be on?

Girls   Father!

Father   Use your scarf as a blindfold Baptista.

Baptista blindfolds her father. They surround him in a circle

Girls   Catch me Father. Here I am (etc).

Father   Watch out. Here I come.

He reaches out for them. The atmosphere is of excitement and fun. The father calls out as he tries to find the girls

> Constantia! Where are you? I am coming for you Constantia!

Suddenly the light and atmosphere changes. The music stops abruptly. A single spot picks out the father. The girls fade into the shadows. The father's hands are forced behind his back as if bound and he drops to his knees. He is in pain

> Constantia! Constantia! (Screaming) Constantia!

The lights change and return to the mother asleep at the table. She jerks up right with a gasp. She reaches out and lights the candle. Her dream has turned to a nightmare and she is afraid

Constantia   No. I will look for you at the Festival Ramon.
                    Please God, may I find you there.

She stands and takes the candle with her as she exits. The ghosts enter once more to watch her depart

Ghost 1   You cling to your light Mother.

Ghost 2   As you cling to your hope.

Ghost 3   Because the darkness is too much to bear.

Ghost 2	But even you Mother . . .
Ghost 1	. . . even you . . .
Ghost 3	. . . at least see the darkness.

·6·

Baptista and Ernesto

Baptista and Ernesto enter the arena space

Baptista	Thank you so much for taking me Ernesto.
Ernesto	You were not bored I hope?
Baptista	Did I seem bored?
Ernesto	Actually – no. You seemed to enjoy yourself.
Baptista	I did. Do you think I said too much Ernesto? I could not help it. The words just flew out of my mouth before I could stop them.
Ernesto	That is what a meeting is for. To talk. To say what you think.
Baptista	I didn't embarrass you?
Ernesto	Not at all. I was proud to be with you.
Baptista	But I did get carried away.
Ernesto	Perhaps a little.
They laugh	
Baptista	It was good to be with people who care. Who want to do something. I did think there would be more.

Ernesto	The people do care but they are afraid. There can be a risk in coming to these meetings Baptista. Terrible things happen.
Baptista	My father used to come to such meetings I think.
Ernesto	I have heard the rumours about your father.
Baptista	He is with the *desaparecidos* Ernesto. The missing, I am sure of it. He will not return. My mother can not accept it. She waits night after night for him.
Ernesto	I am sorry. I am sure that he was a brave and good man Baptista.
Baptista	He was Ernesto.
Ernesto	Perhaps, I should not have brought you here.
Baptista	No. I wanted to come. I want to be involved Ernesto.
Ernesto	(*Uncertain of what she means*) Involved?
Baptista	I cannot watch what is happening and do nothing.
Ernesto	Oh I see. You should not rush into this Baptista. Come to some more meetings and hear more of what we do before you make up your mind. It can be dangerous to join with us.
Baptista	I think we live in a dangerous world Ernesto. I cannot be like my mother. It is as if she cannot look beyond the walls of the house. She refuses to see what is happening. She buries her head in the sand and tries to make

it all go away. I'm sorry. Thank you for walking me to the bus. I hope you have not had to go out of your way.

Ernesto   Not at all. It's been a pleasure.

Baptista   Well, goodnight then.

Ernesto   Baptista, perhaps if you are free on Saturday we could do this again?

Baptista   Another meeting?

Ernesto   Well . . . no. There is a dance – a festival. I thought we could go. Possibly.

Baptista   I will think about it Ernesto.

Ernesto   (*With a slight resignation, feeling he may have been rejected*) Right, well I will see you in work tomorrow. Goodnight.

Baptista   Goodnight Ernesto.

They shake hands a little awkwardly and Baptista exits

Ernesto   A four mile walk home, Ernesto. I hope she is worth it.

He makes to leave when Baptista returns

Baptista   The answer is yes Ernesto.

She quickly kisses him

Baptista   Goodnight.

She exits. He smiles, celebrates 'his success' and exits. The ghosts enter the space he has left

Ghost 1   A flower blooms in the dead of the night.

Ghost 2   But love is not enough.

Ghost 3	Love is never enough.
Ghost 2	And in the reed beds, far upstream. A hidden form loses its shackles and rises slowly, dreamily to the surface.
Ghost 3	A memory to haunt the living . . .
Ghost 1	Begins its final journey to join the dead.

·7·

The Fishwives

Catalina and Juanita enter. They have laundry baskets with them. During this scene the fishwives advance across the arena space hanging washing on the lines that have dropped into place

Catalina	Wash, wash wash. Sometimes, Juanita, that is all I seem to do. For all the thanks I get, I think the only reason that I have a family is to provide me with washing to do.
Juanita	I know what you mean, Juanita. But at least our sheets are clean – not like that Maria Sanchez. I don't know how she has the nerve to hang those out where people can see.
Catalina	A good boiling. That's what they need.
Juanita	And her too! Gossip, gossip, gossip. That's all she ever does. Always talking behind people's backs and not a good word for anyone.
Catalina	Just like that Anita Rodriguez.

Juanita	And Carlotta Estobar.
Catalina	Terrible people. They should keep their opinions to themselves.

Dolores and Carmen enter

Dolores	Good morning Catalina. Juanita.

They both say good morning

Juanita	We were just saying about that Maria Sanchez.
Carmen	The sheets?
Catalina	The sheets.
All	Ay ay ay ay!
Catalina	How are you today Dolores?
Dolores	I can't complain. My back aches. My knees are swollen and my neck is stiff but apart from that and being married to Jose – I am fine.
Juanita	And you Carmen?
Carmen	That Inez – Isadora's girl. She is making eyes at my Alfredo again. I keep on telling him. She is not good enough for you. Only the best for my sons. But him. When she smiles at him he drools like a puppy after its food. A pretty face and a shapely leg and he becomes an idiot.
Catalina	Men will be men Carmen.
Dolores	Men will be boys you mean. My Jose spends all day ogling these young things then comes to me at night with his . . . demands. I'm just not up to it anymore.

Juanita	Men and their demands. Out all day, a smoke and a drink, two minutes of pleasure.
Carmen	For them!
Juanita	And then six hours of snoring.

There is general agreement with these sentiments

Catalina	Well since my Roberto passed away, at least I don't have that sort of trouble. Not that I wouldn't mind some. Tell your Alfredo to watch out. There are some things that a young man is good for. Perhaps I will come knocking on his door.

There is general mirth and merriment

Juanita	Perhaps the best kind of husband is the dead kind!
Dolores	Better six feet under than flopping around on top!
Carmen	Talking of dead husbands, have you seen Constantia.
Catalina	Not for days.
Dolores	She never was one for mixing but now . . .
Juanita	Stand-offish, that's her.
Carmen	We should only speak of her with kindness now. She still thinks that her Ramon is going to come back. She puts a candle in the window for him every night.
Catalina	Well, she will have to come to terms with it sooner or later. He's dead. We all know it. She has to get on with her life.

Dolores	That is easier said than done, Catalina. How can she mourn her husband without a body. At least you know that Roberto is in his grave. All she knows is that Ramon went out one night and has not returned.
Juanita	He is dead though isn't he?
Carmen	I heard that the men saw him leave the cantina and that two policemen went out after him. Nothing was thought of it at the time.
Catalina	Someone heard a car, I think.
Dolores	He was a good man her Ramon. He always spoke his mind. He stood for what is right. But he should have been more careful. Now his family is left without a father and Constantia is without a husband.
Juanita	You have to be careful what you say. A word these days and you can wind up. (*She draws her finger across her throat*)
Catalina	In a world of lies, there is no wisdom in speaking the truth.
Carmen	Then how does the world change?
Catalina	For us Carmen, it doesn't. The world is as it is. We cannot change it. For us there will be peace in the next world but this life is to be endured.
Juanita	I hear that one of her daughters is going the same way.
Carmen	Baptista?
Juanita	That's the one. She is courting some young firebrand from the town.

Catalina	She takes after her father that one.
Juanita	Mixing with a boy from the town is not good. There will be trouble there.
Catalina	But when you look at the men here, then who can blame her!

There is general agreement. The atmosphere lifts

Dolores	Well someone needs to talk to Constantia. She can't go on like this. For the good of the family she must look to her daughters and count her blessings.
Catalina	Perhaps I will talk to her. My Roberto was not like her Ramon but I might be able to help.
Carmen	That would be a kindness Catalina.
Catalina	Perhaps.
Juanita	Did you grieve a lot for Roberto?
Catalina	Oh yes Juanita – but it got a lot easier after the first five minutes.

They all laugh. They have finished hanging out the washing and with continued banter they exit.

·8·

The Festival

Ernesto and Baptista enter from opposite ends of the arena. They cannot see each other because of the washing

Ernesto	Baptista! Baptista!

Baptista	Ernesto? Where are you?
Ernesto	Here I am Baptista.

The lines of washing raise to reveal Baptista and Ernesto. The washing is now the flags and banners of the festival. Ernesto and Baptista embrace

Ernesto	I am sorry that I am late. We had to have a special meeting. You know about the injuries at the factory today.
Baptista	Yes. Poor Consuella. She was such a pretty girl.
Ernesto	Not any more.
Baptista	No.

Others now begin to enter, forming into groups. Music begins to play

Ernesto	But we will do something Baptista. There is to be a workers' march through the town to the corporation offices. There we will make speeches and protest.
Baptista	Will it do any good?
Ernesto	Who knows. There will be newsmen there. If it is shown on American television, perhaps we can shame the owners into doing something. Every little helps.
Baptista	I will be there Ernesto.
Ernesto	I knew you would be. Now, let us be happy! It is a beautiful evening and the crowds are gathering.
Baptista	I love the festival time.
Ernesto	A time for singing and a time for dancing. I will sweep you off your feet tonight Baptista. I hope you have brought your dancing shoes!

Baptista	When I dance, for a moment I can forget about everything else.
Ernesto	The spirit of the people is in the dance Baptista.
Baptista	One thing Ernesto. My mother and my sisters are here tonight. I still have not told Mother about you.
Ernesto	Then we will tell her tonight. It has been almost a month now Baptista. I would not want to be seen as less than honorable in your mother's eyes.
Baptista	Tonight then.
Girl	Baptista! Ernesto! Over here. The dancing will begin soon!

Others also call to them. Baptista and Ernesto go over to them. A pause.
Constantia and Francisca enter. They do not see Baptista

Francisca	There are many people here tonight. It is good to see such happiness.
Constantia	It is Francisca. It is good to see people in high spirits.
Francisca	And you Mother?
Constantia	I thought that perhaps your father might come back tonight.
Francisca	Mother . . .
Constantia	Do not worry Francisca. I am not gloomy.
Girl	(*Calling*) Francisca!
Constantia	Go to them Francisca. Enjoy yourself.

Francisca goes over to the other girls. The Mother drinks in the atmosphere.
Catalina begins to approach her

Constantia   (*To herself*) Well, Ramon?

Catalina   Good evening to you Constantia.

Constantia   Good evening Catalina.

Catalina   How are you keeping Constantia?

Constantia   I am well thank you. And yourself?

Catalina   Oh you know how it is Constantia. On an
                    evening such as this I almost miss my Roberto.
                    Almost. It must be hard for you, without
                    Ramon. Have you had any news dear?

Constantia   No.

Catalina   No? Well if you ever need a shoulder. I am
                    always here.

Constantia   I am sure you are, Catalina.

Catalina   Grief is such a burden to bear on your
                    own.

Constantia   I am not grieving Catalina. Ramon will be back
                    soon.

Catalina   Well, they say there is always room for
                    optimism.

Constantia   If you will excuse me Catalina, I . . .

Catalina   There was one thing Constantia.

Constantia   Yes.

Catalina   Now I'm not trying to interfere or anything
                    like that but with things being the way they
                    are I felt I just had to say something.

Constantia	About?
Catalina	This Ernesto that your Baptista is seeing. Now I know that he is handsome and everyone says he is a good boy but he is one of these political people. Goes to meetings. Stirs up trouble Constantia.
	Do you think it's wise to let it go on? I mean, it could be your Ramon all over again couldn't it. He always spoke his mind and look where it got him. Your family doesn't need any more trouble now does it.
	You do know about Baptista and this Ernesto don't you? They haven't been carrying on behind your back?
Constantia	(*Hesitates*) Of course I know about Baptista and . . . Thank you for your concern Catalina but there is no need to worry.
Catalina	Are you sure Constantia. You can't just ignore these things you know.
Constantia	This is a family matter Catalina. I am sure you understand.
Catalina	Of course. Well you know where I am.
Constantia	Yes. Goodnight Catalina.
Catalina	Goodnight Constantia.

Catalina moves off. Constantia stands for a moment and then exits seeking Baptista. Music plays louder and the crowd exits to dance. The ghosts enter the space

Ghost 1	And in the reed beds far upstream.
Ghost 2	Carried by the rain swollen water.

Ghost 3	A form breaks free . . .
Ghost 1	. . . and begins the journey home.

Everyone bursts in to the space which is now where they dance. There is an atmosphere of excitement and happiness

Maria	I like Ernesto, Baptista. He is nice.
Baptista	And he is mine Maria!
Francisca	But you must tell Mother soon Baptista. It is wrong to keep this from her.
Baptista	I will tell her at the end of the Festival tonight. Ernesto wants to be introduced to her.

Ernesto approaches

Ernesto	It is almost time for the last dance.
Maria	It has been a wonderful evening.
Francisca	Yes it has.

Music begins to play and there are calls for Ernesto to lead the dance. He does so. He then draws Baptista in to dance with him. The others gradually join in until all are dancing. The mood is of celebration as all gloom is lost in the dance. Towards the end Constantia enters to watch. At the end Baptista and Ernesto kiss. Constantia looks on

Constantia	Baptista!
Baptista	Mother!

She takes Ernesto by the hand and leads him over to Constantia. The other dancers gather in a group lost in their own happiness

Baptista	Mother, I am sorry. I should have told you before. We did not mean to keep anything from you. This is . . .

Constantia	Ernesto, yes I know. Baptista, what do you mean by . . .

There is a sudden commotion amongst the crowd. There is some shock and confusion. Maria and Francisca hug each other

Constantia	What is it? Ramon?
Woman	To the river, Constantia. You must come to the river now.
Constantia	Oh dear God. Ramon. Is it Ramon?
Woman	Now Constantia, come now.

Constantia and the others exit as the flags and banners fall to the ground, leaving just the ghosts standing almost accusingly facing the audience.

·9·

The River of Death

Ghost 1	Over the rocks and through the rapids . . .
Ghost 2	. . . carried by the current . . .
Ghost 3	. . . lifeless and limp . . .
Ghost 1	. . . bloated and swollen . . .
Ghost 2	. . . comes the body.
Ghost 3	Her one and only true love borne by the waters of life . . .
Ghost 1	. . . now the river of death.
Ghost 2	Battered and broken.
Ghost 3	The corpse that once held his spirit . . .

Ghost 1	. . . now vacant, inert empty . . .
Ghost 2	. . . but the signs of his passing are there.
Ghost 3	The gashes where he was bound at the wrists.
Ghost 1	The slices through his chest and legs . . .
Ghost 2	. . . the bruises and the shattered limbs . . .
Ghost 3	. . . all from before . . .
Ghost 1	. . . before he went into the water.
Ghost 2	And the holes where the bullets took half his face.
Ghost 3	The half that is left, twisted in pain horror and fear.
Ghost 1	But enough left . . .
Ghost 2	. . . enough left to tell her that this is . . .
Ghost 3	. . . her husband.

Music begins to play. The shattered body of the father is carried into the arena. It is half funeral procession, half the drifting of the body down the river. The body is brought to the ground and 'washed up against the shore'. (See performance notes)

Constantia approaches the body. She kneels beside it then lifts the head, gently, lovingly into her lap

Constantia   (*Whispering as if trying to wake him*) Ramon?

The scene switches to the Dream Mother who is cradling the Father in her lap in exactly the same way. He is asleep

D. Mother   Ramon. Ramon!

Father   What is it?

D. Mother   It is time we were going Ramon.

Father	Really mother?
D. Mother	The girls are playing in the field. They will be exhausted after today.
Father	They have enjoyed themselves. The procession was tremendous this year. And did we dance today Constantia!
D. Mother	We did Ramon. My shoes are almost worn through.
Father	I love you Constantia.
D. Mother	I love you Ramon.

She kisses him tenderly

Father	I will not be coming home Constantia.
D. Mother	I know Ramon.
Father	Now I can be laid at rest and go with them.
D. Mother	I will miss you Ramon.
Father	I will miss you all. In your dreams, Constantia, come here to visit me − not to the river.
D. Mother	I will try. Why did I not know Ramon? About what you did, what you said? Why did you keep it from me?
Father	You did not want to know Constantia. Your world was the house and the children. You were happy.
D. Mother	Perhaps I should have been less happy and known more.
Father	Perhaps.
D. Mother	My heart breaks Ramon.

Father   Goodbye my sweet. Be strong.

He is led gently away into the shadows by the ghosts

D. Mother   Goodbye.

The lights switch back to Constantia

Constantia   (Sobbing) Ramon (*It tears itself from her*) Ramon!

The mother is comforted and the body is taken from the space leaving only the ghosts

Ghost 1   And now she can mourn.

Ghost 3   Now she can grieve.

Ghost 2   Her tears will run until they flood the river that carried her love.

Ghost 1   And for a while the murmurs fade . . .

Ghost 2   . . . and the ghosts depart.

Ghost 3   But if she listens very carefully . . .

Ghost 2   . . . she will hear them whisper . . .

Ghost 1   . . . Baptista. What about Baptista?

·10·

The Mother

Constantia enters with a photograph and places it on the table. She strikes a match and lights a candle. Time has passed

Constantia   I light the candle Ramon. Not to light your way home, but to remember you. You are dead and your body lies in the ground. I pray that you are in heaven. I know from the marks on your body that you went though hell to get there.

I did not think that such things were possible Ramon. I did not think a man could do such harm to another. I know now that you are dead, but I can never know your pain. I pray that my love was of some comfort in your final hours but I feel there can have been little to ease your agony.

And I blame you Ramon. Why was our life not enough? Why did you have to try to right the world as well? Why did you have to speak the truth?

And I blame myself. How could I warn you of the danger when I was blind to it? I thought that love and children and a home would be enough. But it is not. All that has to exist somewhere. And I need to know about that. I have lived my life in a fairy tale. Looking away when the real world thrust itself upon me, forcing myself not to see.

My children live in that real world Ramon. Why should I warn them not to play in the road when I choose not to see the traffic. How can I protect them when I do not know?

She exits and there is a blackout.

·11·

A Death

Ernesto and Baptista enter the arena space laughing

Baptista   It is a beautiful night Ernesto.

Ernesto   And you are beautiful too.

Baptista   You flatter me Ernesto.

Ernesto   I speak the truth. I thought you were a little sad tonight.

Baptista   It is Mother. Father has been buried for three weeks now Ernesto but she seems to have aged thirty years.

Ernesto   Time will heal her. But she will never forget.

Baptista   It was a good meeting tonight. You spoke well.

Baptista   Do you think that the protest march did any good?

Ernesto   There were more people than I thought there would be. It went well. The cameras were there.

Baptista   Your speech helped a lot. You spoke with passion. It made people want to do something.

Ernesto   They say I was on the news. It felt good to do it Baptista.

Baptista   I am proud of you Ernesto.

Ernesto   Baptista, marry me.

Baptista   Ernesto!

Ernesto   I know it is sudden and not the right time but there is never a right time. I love you Baptista. Marry me.

Baptista   I do not know what to say Ernesto.

Ernesto   You could try just saying yes.

Baptista   Ernesto, I . . .

There is a movement and two figures who have been watching emerge from the darkness

Shadow 1   Ernesto Ortega?

Ernesto   Yes?

The shadows pull guns. Two shots are fired and Ernesto falls backwards. As he crawls on his hands and knees, a third shot is fired and he lies still.

Baptista   Ernesto? (*Shouts as she falls on her knees beside his body*) Ernesto!

Shadow 2   Shut up you bitch!

He swings his foot viciously at her head. She is dazed. They pull her to her feet

Shadow 1   And now we have some fun together eh!

Laughing, they take her away. Music plays as the ghosts enter to raise Ernesto gently to his feet and lead him away. Blackout.

·12·

The News

People enter the space as if gathering in a village square. They talk in hushed tones

Gossip 1   That poor Constantia. First her husband and now this.

Gossip 2	It is a terrible burden. I don't know how she will carry on.
Gossip 3	That Ernesto was a good boy. To be shot down in the street like that.
Gossip 4	At least for him it is over. What has happened to Baptista?
Gossip 1	It does not bear thinking about.
Gossip 2	Who did it do you think? The police?
Gossip 3	Perhaps. Ernesto spoke his mind you see. He stood up for what is right.
Gossip 4	A brave boy. We must say prayers for him tonight.
Gossip 1	And for Baptista.
Gossip 2	From what they say, she may have most need of them.

The focus switches to another group

Gossip 5	The body was all cut to pieces they say. Blood everywhere.
Gossip 6	Who do they think did it?
Gossip 7	Drug dealers. That's what I heard.
Gossip 6	I thought Ernesto was a good boy.
Gossip 5	I've heard he was a police informer.

The focus switches to another group

Gossip 8	Found in each others arms they were.
Gossip 9	You mean she is dead! I thought they did not find her body.

Gossip 10   I thought it was she who killed him.

Gossip 8   But they were in love.

Gossip 10   I thought she was protecting him from the bullets?

The focus switches to the first group

Gossip 1   I have heard that drugs were involved.

Gossip 3   I do not believe that. They were good children.

Gossip 2   Who is to know these things.

Gossip 4   They are a good family.

The focus switches to the second group

Gossip 5   So he was pimping for her was he. Who would have thought.

Gossip 6   There was this whole gang. Raped her and dumped her in the sea.

Gossip 7   A terrible end.

Gossip 5   What can you expect when you are involved in such things.

The focus switches to the third group

Gossip 8   Perhaps they were just in the wrong place at the wrong time.

Gossip 9   I'm sure they have not found her.

Gossip 10   No, no. She is dead for certain.

Gossip 8   Look, here comes Constantia.

Constantia and Francisca enter

Gossip 1   Our hearts are with you Constantia.

Gossip 2	And our prayers.
Gossip 3	Is there any news Constantia?
Francisca	There is nothing new. Baptista is still missing.
Constantia	We have been to the police. They say it was a gangland killing. They say if the gang has taken Baptista then they may ransom her. But what is the point. We have no money.
Gossip 4	Do you trust the police Constantia?
Constantia	I do not know. Who can you trust?
Gossip 9	Do you think Baptista is still alive Constantia?
Constantia	I pray that she is.
Francisca	Come along Mother, we should go inside.
Constantia	I want to talk to them Francisca. Find out what they know.
Francisca	Mother, they are terrible gossips. Some say bad things. It will do no good.
Constantia	I did not listen to them about your father, but some knew. Amongst the lies may be grains of truth. I will not do nothing Francisca. I have to try.

They approach some of the other women who offer comfort. Maria and Isabel enter

Isabel	Mother, Mother. We have news.

Everyone gathers around them

Maria	There was a man at our house.
Isabel	He was in the same group that Ernesto belonged to.

Gossip	A drug dealer!
Constantia	No. Ernesto had no dealings with drugs.
Gossip	Who is to say what he may . . .
Constantia	I am to say. Ernesto was a good man. Do not blacken his name with lies.
Maria	The man said, they have someone who works for the police who lets them know what goes on.
Gossip	An informer.
Isabel	He says that a woman was taken to a prison in another town that night. He is sure it was Baptista.
Constantia	Then she is alive.
Maria	She was alive when she arrived Madre. Beaten but alive.
Constantia	Then I must go to her. But why did the police not tell me about this?
Maria	They do not want you to know Madre.
Francisca	These prisons Madre. Are terrible places. You must not hope too much.
Constantia	But I may hope a little Francisca. That is enough. I will go to the police again. I will try to find my Baptista. I will not sit at home as I did with your father. Come.

They exit to good wishes from the gossips

Gossip	I have heard of what happens in these prisons.
Gossip	Perhaps it would have been better to have found her body, than to have had such news.

·13·

The Search/The Prison

In the centre of the room, on a chair, sits Baptista. Her hands and feet are bound. She is blindfolded and has been beaten

Baptista   Oh my Lord, help me. Bring me to my mother's arms. To my love's sweet embrace. I am hurting. God I am hurting. I hurt so much.

Scene switches to the mother and Francisca approaching an official

Official 1   Wait there

Constantia   I am sorry. Is this the right office for . . .

Official 1   There. Wait there.

Constantia   But I'm looking for . . .

Official 1   Are you trouble makers?

Francisca   What?

Official 1   Are you trying to cause trouble?

Francisca   No. No. It's just. We are only . . .

Official 1   Do you want me to call for the security guards?

Constantia   Security?

Official 1   This is a busy office. You can see all the paper work I have to do. And you come in here making difficulties. Causing disruption. I work for the government. I do the work of the government and you come in here and think you can upset the smooth running of my office?

The scene switches back to Baptista

Baptista   Blood is seeping out of my body like running
                      water. My eyes ache. My ears sting. My mouth
                      bleeds. Ernesto. They won't tell me. What has
                      happened to you Ernesto?

The scene switches back to the mother

Constantia   The woman outside told us to come in.

Official 2   Are you a subversive? Come in here to spread
                      your communist filth. To spread your filthy
                      lies. To preach rebellion. Is that it? You're one
                      of these traitors who wants to betray our
                      president. Betray your own country. Your
                      mother country? Is that who you are? Is it?

Constantia   (Quietly) No. (*A moment*) I'm a mother. I'm
                      looking for my daughter. She went missing
                      three nights ago. They say the police took her.

Official   You want another office. This is a prison
                      matter. Try there.

The scene switches to Baptista.

Baptista   Please leave me alone. Don't touch me. Please.
                      Please. I am hurting so much. Is there anyone
                      there? Is there anyone the ... (*She screams in pain*)

The scene switches to the mother with another official

Official 3   Do you have a form?

Constantia   A form. No, I don't have a form. Nobody said
                      anything about a form. Why didn't anybody
                      tell me about a form?

Official 3   You need a form. You need to go to another
                      office.

Constantia	Can't you just . . .
Official 3	I need a form. Now do you want a form or do you want me to call a guard?
Francisca	Which form do we ask for?
Official 3	There's only one.

The scene switches

Baptista	I am so alone. I try to numb myself. Try to escape my body and fly. But the pain brings me back. And they laugh. Laugh as they hurt me. Laugh as they touch me. Feel me. Ask if I like what they do. (*Hearing approaching footsteps*) They are coming again. I want to die.

The scene switches

Official 4	Which form do you want?
Francisca	They said there was just one.
Official 4	Oh no. We have lots of forms. You need to know which one.
Constantia	Will you tell us?
Official 4	Try the office down the corridor.

The scene switches

Baptista	It cannot be much longer now. The time of my release. The time of my escape. (*Suddenly terrified. She has heard a noise*) What is that sound? What is it? (*screams in agony*)

The scene switches

Official 5	But this is in another town.
Francisca	Does that make a difference?

Official 5	Of course. I cannot deal with this.
Constantia	Then what do I do?
Official 5	You will have to go there.
Francisca	But that is twenty miles away.
Official 5	It is where it is. I cannot help that.
Constantia	I have been to eight offices in the last three days. Could I not have been told this at the start.
Official 5	Constantia Diaz, isn't it?
Constantia	That's right.
Official 5	Your husband, Ramon. He was a trouble maker too was he not. It seems that you are the same.
Constantia	I just want to know.
Official 5	Know what?
Constantia	The truth.
Official 5	But this is the government! I hope you find your daughter.

The scene switches

Baptista	Yes Ernesto . . . Yes.

Baptista's head drops. Music plays. The ghosts emerge from the shadows. They gently untie her, tenderly raise her to her feet and lead her away.

·14·

The Fight goes on

The mother and her daughters are gathered at the table

Maria   Madre, you are exhausted. You must rest.

Constantia   I cannot rest until I know. I will try again
                    tomorrow. I will not stop looking for her.

Isabel   But what more can you do? They tell us
                    nothing.

Constantia   Then I can at least ask the questions. I have met
                    so many other women: wives, mothers, even
                    grandmothers who have suffered as we have. I
                    did not know any of this before. Their grief is
                    my grief now.

Francisca   You cannot take the world on your shoulders
                    Madre. Madre, I am pregnant. I want my child
                    to meet its grandmother.

Constantia   Francisca. This is good news. So your Basilio is
                    a man after all.

They all laugh

Constantia   Be a better mother than me Francisca.

Francisca   Madre. You are the best mother there can be.

Constantia   No. No, I am not. I thought that all I had to do
                    was wash and keep the house and home. Cook
                    and clean, mend, hold your hands and patch
                    your knees when you fall. But that is not
                    enough. Love is not enough.

                    Your father protected me from the world and I

was happy to live in that bubble. But you live in that world. And in that world is violence and cruelty and pain. I cannot be a mother to my children unless I am a mother to the world as well.

Maria   You cannot change the world Madre.

Constantia   I can at least know what needs changing and let others know what I know. If I do that then I have changed the world a little.

Tomorrow I will I go to the town square and join with the other mothers and wives of the missing. And we will dance.

Isabel   Dance mother?

Constantia   Yes – dance, my sweet. I will dance with Ramon and Baptista. But I will dance alone. I will remember them and help others not to forget.

·15·

They Dance Alone

The women form into lines across the space. They all have a photograph of their loved ones pinned to their clothes. One by one they say

Woman   I dance with . . . (*Each names a missing person, their relationship to them and a brief message or prayer. Ideally these should be actual disappeared or imprisoned people. See Performance Notes*)

Finally the mother speaks

Constantia   I dance with Ramon and Baptista. Ramon, my husband, murdered by the police for saying what he thought. Baptista, my daughter, taken by the police. May she come home soon.

Music plays and they begin to dance alone. Having established the dance as it proceeds, one by one the women begin to exit — still moving in time to the music. As they do this a procession of Ramon, Ernesto and Baptista each carrying a candle slowly enters flanked by the ghosts. They position themselves around Constantia. The light slowly fades until a tight spot barely illuminates the mother's face supported by the light from the candles. As the music begins to fade away Constantia stops dancing

Constantia   Ramon. Baptista I love you.

Ramon, Ernesto and Baptista blow out their candles. Blackout.

PERFORMANCE MATERIALS

Set

A Mother's Voice can be staged in a variety ways but was originally presented on a thrust stage with the audience placed on three sides. A large table, covered with a white table cloth and surrounded by six chairs was in an isolated area upstage, backed by curtaining. This area represented the 'house' and off-stage areas to each side of this space were used as entrances to the house and to conceal the limited number of props used.

The large remaining rectangular area provided the open space needed for most of the performance. This had exit and entry points for the cast at each corner. During the performance the cast did not exit the auditorium but would position themselves in unlit areas behind the audience when they were not on stage.

Although it would be possible to mime the hanging out of the washing in the fishwives scene it is more effective if three or four lines can be strung on pulleys across the main space. These can be lowered into position to enable the fish wives to hang out their washing – which consists of rectangular pieces of cloth (roughly the size of tea towels) dyed in a variety of colours.

Following this scene the lines remain down until Ernesto and Baptista enter. They lose sight of each other in the avenues of washing but on cue the lines can be pulled back up and they then become the flags and bunting of the festival which follows. These are then released to fall into the main area and be cleared away as Constantia rushes out followed by the other villagers on the news of the discovery of the father's body.

The effect is simple yet impressive although much depends on having adequate head room in your auditorium.

Props

Only a limited number of props are needed. Place settings will be needed for the table and bowls of bread and fruit can serve to represent the meal. The fishwives will need their washing, washing baskets and clothes pegs. A special chair should be prepared with straps fitted to hold Baptista for the torture scene. A number of other incidental items such as framed photographs for the mother will be needed.

On several occasions candles are lit and carried on the stage. It is vital that permission for the use of naked flames on stage is obtained from your local fire officer and certain restrictions may apply. Costumes and drapes that may come into contact with a candle must be flameproofed to the required standard. Fire buckets should be positioned in the off stage areas to douse the candle flames in.

You will also require one or two blank firing pistols for use by the shadows in the murder scene.

Costume

Costume is mostly simple and straightforward. Although suggestive of Central and South America it is essentially a mix of the 'ethnic' rural and urban. In the original performance the female costume was simply loose skirts and blouses with flat shoes. The father wore a plain jacket and trousers which was duplicated by the 'body'. Ernesto wore a jean and jacket combination. For the shadows (gunmen) appropriate (slightly Americanised) 'street' wear would be suitable. For the 'officials', members of the cast wore formal coats or jackets over their costumes. They should appear as distant civil servants.

The Ghosts were dressed in tattered and worn versions of the female costumes, suggesting their own deaths. They were barefooted and their make up made them appear pale and drawn with dishevelled hair. However care was taken to make their costumes not so radically different from the other costumes that they could not 'blend in' when needed. If this is not a requirement of your production then you could produce a more radical costume design.

The person playing the 'body' of the father must wear a face mask as the actual father appears in the same scene. This can be blank or mirror the description of the father's face in death given by the ghosts.

PERFORMANCE EXERCISES

These exercises are meant to introduce a performance group to *A Mother's Voice* and some of the demands it is likely to make upon them. The first exercise (used in the original production) is intended to enable the performers to make an emotional connection between themselves and the subject matter of the piece. The subsequent exercises help to either enhance the bonding of the group or to focus them on particular methods of presentation.

The Conscience Wall

Many of the performers may have very little knowledge of 'Prisoners of Conscience', disappearances, torture or the systematic repression of the citizens of a country by state or military machinery. To bring truth and honesty to their work the performers need to gain a personal insight to the situation they are depicting through the use of research. During rehearsals it is worthwhile creating opportunities for the group to share and discuss what they have uncovered and their own feelings in relation to it.

In the original production we created a 'Wall of Conscience' to which all those involved in the production contributed. This was a collection of articles, pictures, stories, poems and cold facts gathered during the rehearsal process. New material was presented or read to the group on a regular basis and then placed on the 'Wall'. This then became part of a display accompanying the performance and a source of inspiration during the rehearsal period. In the original production five free-standing display boards were covered in this way over a period of two weeks.

Trust

All trust exercises require care from those involved and close supervision from the group leader.

Exercise A

The whole group disperse themselves about the space and stand in absolute silence. They then close their eyes. One member of the group is then given the task of 'finding' the others. They move slowly and carefully around the space until they contact another person. The contacted person then places an outstretched hand on the shoulder of the 'finder' and follows on behind. This continues until all members of the group have been located and joined on to the line.

If at any point it is proving hard to locate remaining individuals then the finder can call out 'Where are you?'. Those not yet joined on can call out once only 'Over here' in reply.

Exercise B

The whole group again stand in the space with their eyes closed. Then slowly and carefully they must try to arrange themselves in a line in height order in the centre of the space. They may talk but not open their eyes whilst doing so. When each considers themselves to be in the right place then they must raise their hands. The group leader can conclude the exercise when all hands are raised.

As a variation you can try this exercise in silence!

Exercise C

This is a silent exercise. The group are divided up into A's and B's. A's stand with their eyes closed. B's are then given the task of slowly guiding A's safely around the room with no bumps or collisions. They guide their partners from behind with one hand gently layed on the shoulder of their partner. Whenever they wish, B's may 'park' their partners by tapping them twice on the shoulder. A must then carefully raise his or her hands and stand still until another B takes over. This should continue for three to four minutes then swap around with A's guiding B's.

Exercise D

Divide into small groups of three to five persons. They are to imagine that they are standing on a piece of paper with a camera overhead. As the group leader calls out numbers and letters they must form themselves into the shape of the number or letter as seen from above. They should only be allowed about 15 seconds before they are told to freeze. After assessing the success of each group another number or letter is called out. Keep this exercise fast and frenetic!

As a variation try this with the whole group working together.

Language

A Mother's Voice is set in Latin America. To avoid the pitfalls of the cast using an accent, to capture the 'foreign' nature of the piece, it has been written using deliberately formal expression and – apart from in one or two places – avoids the use of contractions. At first the cast may be struck by the 'strangeness' of the language, however, they must be able to speak fluently, naturally and conversationally in this style.

Exercise A

Divide into small groups (three is ideal). One person is to act as a judge whilst the others have to sustain a fluent conversation. The role of the judge is to spot anyone using contractions (for example I'm instead of I am, it's instead of it is) in their speech. Once spotted, and the error pointed out, the judge enters the conversation and the 'sinner' becomes the judge.

Exercise B

In small groups improvise a typical scene from a well-known television soap opera. Try to use an appropriate accent but do not use contractions. This exercise can really heighten the cast's awareness of the way language is used in *A Mother's Voice*.

Dance

Dance is used frequently in *A Mother's Voice*. This is not the choreographed and polished dance of the musical, however, but the robust, energetic and raw dance of everyday people celebrating a vital part of their lives and culture. It is essential that the cast should not just be at ease with this, but positively enjoy this element of their work!

Try to fill rehearsal sessions with the music of the piece. It is a good idea to use music at the beginning and end of the session. In the original production every session concluded with the whole group dancing to a set piece of music.

Exercise A

Divide the group up into pairs and label them A or B then play a suitable piece of music. At first A must devise and 'teach' a simple dance movement suited to the music to B. B must then do the same to A. After a while they must break up and find different partners to whom they must teach the move they were taught (not the move they devised). This then repeats with them continually learning new moves and teaching them to new partners.

Exercise B

Arrange the group in a circle then label the group alternately A and B. A's then turn to the left and B's to the right. They are now facing dancing partners. To appropriate music they dance with their partners until told to move on by the group leader. A's and B's then move on to their next partner around the circle. When everyone has danced with everyone else then the whole group should dance together.

Relaxation

Working on *A Mother's Voice* can be an intense and emotionally draining experience. There may be times when the whole cast will need to be 'diffused' or individuals may need to focus themselves. These exercises can be for the whole group or the individual.

Exercise A

Lie down on the floor with your eyes closed. Try to visualise yourself lying on a beach. Without altering your position press down as if trying to make an imprint of your body in the sand. Become aware of all the points of contact your body is making with the floor.

After a while stop pressing down and try to 'release' each point of contact. Visualise that on your body you are gradually tying helium filled balloons. As you tie on more balloons try to feel the point of contact lift. Keep on focusing on this until in your imagination you can see yourself suspended a few centimetres above the surface of the beach. After a few minutes imagine the balloons slowly deflating and laying you gently back down. Stay in this position and try to empty your mind for a few minutes before slowly sitting up and opening your eyes.

Exercise B

Sit upright on a chair with your eyes closed. Hands and arms should be relaxed. Focus on your breathing, inhaling through your nose and exhaling through your mouth. Inhale to a mental count of 5 and hold the breath for a moment before releasing in a careful and controlled way through the mouth to a count of 10–15.

As you breathe in and out try to visualise the 'journey' the air takes through your body. Give the air a colour as you breathe it in. In your lungs imagine it turning another colour which you then exhale. Continue the exercise for 3–5 minutes.

PERFORMANCE NOTES AND EXERCISES

The Ghosts

Throughout the play there is a mix of the real world, the dream world and the 'spirit' world. The Ghosts stand at the intersection between those three worlds. They represent dying, death and the passage into the world beyond. They are the guardians of the dead and their guides to the hereafter. They mourn, however, for the living: angered by their complacency and driven to despair by their naivety.

They are 'human' in form yet elemental in their passion. Their movement and vocal delivery should echo this. The Ghosts need to be performed with energy, dynamism and a heightened degree of intensity. They are three – yet they are one.

Exercise 1

This is a physical exploration exercise to help the actors playing the Ghosts discover how to use the space and develop their individual movement. Each should stand perfectly still in a large open space with their feet close together. Slowly they should allow themselves to lean in a certain direction. As they begin to lose their balance they should move in that direction until they can recover their starting position. They should then repeat this again and again, showing awareness of the others in the space and avoiding collisions.

This exercise in loss of control and recovery is a useful way of discovering the free-flowing slightly chaotic nature of the Ghosts. It must be performed with sustained concentration and serious intensity. As a development, music can be introduced and the performers asked to follow the beat whilst 'falling'. They can also imagine themselves as particular animals – lizards with their odd combination of total stillness followed by rapid darting movements are particularly effective.

Exercise 2

You should avoid allowing the Ghosts to become static during
their line delivery. Again the guideline here is stillness followed
by moments of dynamic action. The performers should form an
inward facing circle holding hands. At a moment decided by
themselves, one should release the grip of one of the hands and
lead the rest in a chain which should then reform when the
leader stops. This pattern of break and release is then repeated.
The chain can even weave in and out of itself. Only one grip
should ever break but others may alter their hand grips to
facilitate movements.

As confidence develops the performers can move to having
points of contact rather than holding hands. On a signal all
release their contacts, move around each other only to reform
with new points of contact moments later. Try a never ending
shifting pattern created by the line delivery – as each line is
delivered so a new shape is formed!

* * * * *

The 'dead' in scene 1 must take responsibility for developing
some of their own lines – the 'whispers'. These are the nagging
doubts that are in Constantia's mind about what has happened
to her husband which despite her faith she cannot totally hold
at bay. Imagine the thoughts that could be in Constantia's
head – the thoughts that she fears most. Construct your own
unique 'doubt'. Keep it fairly concise and repeat it over and over
again. Deliver the line as a clearly audible whisper. Work with
the rest of the dead to ensure that no one voice overwhelms any
other.

Exercise 3

When forming the postures of death you need to avoid cliché.
Imagine that you are in extreme pain and locate that pain in a
fixed point in your body. Feel the intensity of the pain and

slowly contract your body towards it. After a few moments, even as you contract begin to resist this and also push away from the source of pain. You should establish a position of total tension which will feel awkward and may appear grotesque. Hold this position and maintain the physical tension as you deliver your lines.

Repeat the exercise vocalising your pain and resistance to the pain at the same time as moving. This can be quite draining!

Absence and Loss

This scene in contrast to the first, is an exercise in naturalism. It is vital to capture the atmosphere of the household and the different qualities of the girls of the house. One of the most difficult moments is Maria's 'breakdown' whilst the mother is absent. This must appear genuine and it is vital that the actress has explored her role fully and developed her understanding of her relationship with her father. In her eyes Maria was always the Father's 'special' girl and she must really feel the pain of his loss at this moment . This is an ideal opportunity to apply some of Stanislavski's ideas on role creation and in particular the application of emotion memory. Maria's weeping must be internally motivated not externally 'performed'.

This scene involves considerable handling of props in the setting of the table. This should flow with the scene and not interrupt it. Therefore, suitable props should be introduced to the rehearsal as soon as possible.

Darkness

Once more in this scene, Constantia slips into the dream world – a world shared by the living and the dead. The father is more animated than in the opening scene yet we should still be aware of a soul in anguish – he is trapped in this twilight world, held captive by his wife's reluctance to accept his death. Lines are 'shared' by Constantia and the Dream Mother. These shared lines help us slip from the real world, into the dream and back again without breaking the continuity.

Exercise 4

A useful practice for this is the 'Alternate word story telling' exercise. This can be performed in pairs or small groups. The aim is to tell a story together with no preplanning, and for each person to contribute a single word at a time. If you think the previous person has reached the end of a sentence then you may say 'Full stop' and give the first word of the next sentence. The aim is to create a flowing narrative that should sound like one story delivered by several voices.

The Factory

The factory scene represents a break from the intensity of the earlier sections and it should raise the atmosphere considerably. The factory girls should be played with life and energy. They maintain their good humour through their camaraderie in the face of long hours and appalling working conditions. Ernesto is an easy target for the girls' humour and an outlet for much of their frustration. They find it easier to tease Ernesto than to face up to the problems they face in the workplace. They feel that nothing will ever change so they may as well get on with life and have what fun they can get.

Exercise 5

During the extended speech by Baptista about the street boy (based on true stories) it is useful if the rest of the girls are quiet and develop a freeze frame. There should be a sense of a moment frozen in time. In preparation for this the cast should experiment with a variety of frozen images which are nonetheless active. They can be divided into groups and asked to devise group images which suggest that:

1. someone has confessed a shocking secret
2. a hilarious joke has just been told
3. they are gossiping about someone in another group
4. someone is being cheered up.

Other ideas can be easily used. These scenes should 'come to life' without hesitation a beat after Baptista's line, 'I have not seen him since'.

The Picnic in the Hills

This visit to Constantia's dreams is to one of her most vivid and happy memories. This should be a depiction of a nearly too perfect familial bliss. The father's zest for life and sheer energy need to be brought out to emphasise the family's loss at his death. He is their heartbeat. Even here, reality intrudes into Constantia's memories and the game of blindman's buff turns into a chilling depiction of Ramon's final moments.

Exercise 6

All of the family are younger in this scene. To encourage a 'wilder' approach, the whole cast should play some familiar childhood games such as 'What's the time Mr Wolf', 'Grandmother's Footsteps' and various tag games. After playing the games as themselves they should play the games again, but as seven year olds, and try to recapture their childish enthusiasm. It can also be useful to spend some time sharing memories of when they really did play such games when they were younger.

Baptista and Ernesto

This is a fairly straightforward episode in which the relationship of the young couple begins to blossom against a background of growing political involvement. It is important that the performers capture the enthusiasm of each character for political justice as well as their slight awkwardness about each other. Ernesto and Baptista remain optimistic about the future but this is countered by the cynical comments of the Ghosts which close the scene.

The Fishwives

The performers can afford to indulge themselves a little with their roles here! The fishwives are the village gossips and should be played with suitable gusto. Be careful though not to exceed the bounds of realism and reduce these characters to superficial stereotypes.

The performers will need to practice the hanging out of the washing with care and precision. The 'washing lines' must be filled by the end of the scene but this must never appear to be the objective.

Exercise 7

The fishwives are flamboyant characters. Their 'gossiping' should be accompanied by suitable gestures, facial expression and posture. In pairs they should try having a conversation as a 'dumbshow' – without using words. They will need to use gesture and mime to ensure that their meaning is made clear. They can then run the same conversation again – this time including both the actions and the dialogue.

Suitable topics could be:

1. the possible fathers of a recently pregnant woman
2. their view on their respective husbands
3. their thoughts about a new family who have moved into the village.

The Festival

The atmosphere in this scene should be one of celebration and excitement. The feeling of vitality and optimism generated should build to a climax in the main dance which concludes with Ernesto and Baptista in an embrace.

The scene needs careful choreography to capture the ebb and

flow of the crowds and to avoid Constantia 'meeting' with
Baptista and Ernesto too soon.

In the original production, the final dance began with a 'solo'
from Ernesto which was then gradually taken up by the rest of
the cast until all (except the mother) were dancing in lines
strung across the arena. In creating the dance we were trying to
create a simple sequence of steps which could be repeated at
ever increasing speed. The music used was a version of
'Sikuriadas' – a traditional Andean song that begins slowly and
becomes wilder and wilder.

Exercise 8

To the music chosen for the main dance, in pairs create a
straightforward sequence of steps. Try to keep the focus on
simple but bold footwork that moves in a rectangular pattern
across the floor. Punctuate each corner of the rectangle with a
firm stamp of the foot. After you have decided on the sequence,
try to follow it together side by side with an outstretched arm
on your partner's shoulder (Zorba the Greek style!). Once you
have mastered this, team up with another pair and try it as a
line of four. As you gain in confidence try to stop looking at
your feet and accompany the accent stamps with vocal shouts!

The River of Death

This can be one of the most moving scenes in the play and is
full of dramatic possibilities. After the introduction by the
Ghosts, the body of the father is brought on stage. As the father
appears later in the scene in a dream sequence, the 'body' will
need to be played by another member of the cast, dressed in a
torn version of the father's costume and suitably masked. The
choice of music here should be solemn and dignified, suitable
for a funeral procession.

Originally the body was brought in held high above the
heads of the carriers. As they progressed into the arena they
moved the body in such a way as to suggest it floating in water

and bouncing off rocks. Eventually the body was carefully placed down as if washed up against the shore. Constantia entered at this point and cradled the head of the body on her lap. In a mirror image the Dream Mother placed the head of the sleeping Ramon in her lap for the farewell dream sequence. During the dream sequence, Constantia, the body and the onlookers (which those involved in the funeral procession became) remained totally frozen.

Exercise 9

Any lifting or carrying work can be very dangerous and must be carefully undertaken. Always practise at first with plenty of crash mats nearby and extra 'catchers' on hand to supply additional help if necessary. This must be closely supervised and the director needs to explain clearly the risks involved and be ready to stop the activity at any time.

You will need to have a group of 'carriers' who are all roughly the same height, the body (choose someone quite light!) and safety catchers. Arrange the carriers behind the body who should be standing up. Assign a carrier one each to the feet, the knees, thighs, the waist, the shoulders and head of the 'body'.

The carriers looking after the feet and knees will have to begin kneeling down. All the carriers will need to be in contact with the body at the point of lifting. They will need to be positioned alternately slightly to the side of the body for the lift. They will move into position directly underneath the body as the lift progresses.

When everyone is ready and with safety catchers and crash mats in position, the body leans backwards keeping themselves straight. As each of the carriers takes the weight of the body they must push upwards and move in underneath. The carriers should stretch out to 'lock' their arms with the body held high above them. Once securely in place the group can then begin to move slowly around the space. After a suitable period reverse the procedure to carefully place the body back on their feet.

Only when the group have practised this several times and are confident can the crash mats be removed. Even in performance, however, the safety catchers can be retained as the funeral entourage. Once comfortable with the basic technique then you can experiment with different movements and transitions to suggest the movement of the body down river. Remember, however that caution and safety must be of paramount importance at all times.

A Death

The opening of this scene should give no indication of what is to follow. Both Ernesto and Baptista are looking forward to the future. The intrusion of the shadows (the gunmen) should be sudden, brief and violent. Be careful not to over-dramatise the shooting of Ernesto which should be done coldly with no passion. Caution needs to be exercised in the use of firearms on stage and in the kick to Baptista which will require careful rehearsal.

The Search / The Prison

This again is a scene of contrasts: the detached cold hostility of the officials is set against the controlled passion of Constantia and the pain and suffering of Baptista. In the original arena style setting, Baptista was placed on a chair in the centre of the space while the officials appeared in the corners of the area. Each space was individually lit and there was space around the seating in the auditorium for Constantia and Francisa to move from one space to the other during Baptista's speeches. By the end of the scene they had quite literally gone in a full circle.

Much of the power of the scene depends on the ability of the actress playing Baptista to honestly capture and portray the pain and terror of her situation. The torturers are deliberately absent but through the performance of Baptista, their presence should be tangible. Any scene as emotional and personal as this requires care and sensitivity during rehearsal.

Exercise 10

To help the actress playing Baptista fully emotionally engage
with this moment, you can use the technique of 'Journeys' to
help fill in the gap between the shooting of Ernesto and the
torture scene. This can help to maintain the Stanislavskian
'through line of action'.

'Journeys' are devised for a single person who is blindfolded
for the duration of the exercise. The rest of the group create a
series of scenes that rely on sound, movement and feeling to
capture a specific experience. They are also responsible for
moving the individual from one scene to the next. A Christmas
journey for instance might begin with carol singers outside a
church on a windy night, move onto a busy street scene of late
night shoppers, on to the unwrapping of Christmas presents
and finish with Christmas crackers and the serving of dinner.
Denied the use of sight the group try to appeal to all the other
senses to bring the experience to life for the 'traveller' – the
sound of tearing paper, being jostled by the crowds and perhaps
even the smell of the dinner! The traveller can be passive or
actively interacting with the scenes.

For Baptista the journey could be broken into these sections:

a) Being bundled into a van and being driven to the prison.
b) Her initial questioning by a police officer (perhaps with others
   watching a football match on TV in the background).
c) She is placed in a holding cell and meets with other prisoners.
d) She is moved again to another cell where she encounters a
   victim of torture. During the course of this piece the other
   prisoner is removed for torture again. She may hear their cries
   of suffering.
e) The door to the cell is opened, she is taken out and strapped
   into the chair.

A word of caution. This can be a very powerful and emotional
exercise and should only be undertaken with the consent of the

actress. At all times she must be assured that she can stop the exercise if she is finding it too intense or does not like what is happening. Take great care to reassure her at all times and be particularly careful when returning her to 'real life'. When deprived of sight and with the particular significance of the blindfold for this situation the imagination can go into overdrive. This exercise can significantly deepen the engagement of the actress with the situation but must only be used if everyone is confident and at ease with it.

They Dance Alone

This scene can be a memorable and emotional experience for both the audience and the cast. If at all possible the names called out by each woman prior to the dance should be those of actual missing people or prisoners of conscience. Hopefully, as part of the research undertaken many actual examples will have been uncovered. Amnesty International is a good source of information for this and can supply details of a number of existing cases.

Each statement should be similar in its pattern, for example: 'I dance with my father Juan Carlos Ortega, taken from our family home on the 15th July 1984 for attending a civil rights meeting. I pray for his safe return.' The actual wording should be decided by the individual actress. Fictional alternatives can be used but knowing that you are dancing for a real person makes these final moments more significant.

Exercise 11

If setting the piece in Latin America then it is highly recommended that the piece of music used is the Andean song 'Dolencias' which has a haunting melody and lilting rhythm.

In the original production the dance was interpreted as a formal courtship dance which might be included in a festival to allow men and women to introduce themselves to each other. With a partner, develop such a dance to appropriate music.

Begin with the man and woman standing opposite each other. Do not allow too much movement across the space – imagine that in the dance the women are in a large circle around a circle of men. They dance with each man for a time before the circle moves on and they dance with a new partner. Work out a sequence of simple moves based on square and try to find ways for the man and woman to swop places and back again. Create a pattern of perhaps no more than six distinct movements which result in the woman returning to her beginning position. The inclusion of a simple spin for the woman can be very effective in the finished dance.

At all times keep eye contact with your partner. Remember that the aim of such a dance is to allow a little flirting between the partners!

Once all the pairs have created a dance, show them to each other and choose elements from each to be included in the final dance. Once this has been decided simply remove the men from the dance so that it is performed by the women alone. You may have to make a few adjustments at this point. The final piece, however, is all the more poignant for having a truly missing partner.

CONTEXT NOTES FOR THE PERFORMER

The Disappeared/Los Desaparecidos

Detentions, torture and summary executions have long been common practices of state terrorism – all over the world. During the 1970s and 80s, however, a new phenomenon emerged in many Central and South American countries as a means of spreading terror throughout society – 'disappearances'. It was particularly evident in Argentina during a six year period known as the 'Dirty War' when over 30,000 people are thought to have 'disappeared'. Thousands more ordinary people 'disappeared' in Chile during the years of General Pinochet's dictatorship. The practice is by no means a uniquely Latin American problem and cases have been reported world-wide, including in Africa, the Middle and Far East and in Central and Eastern Europe.

'Disappearances' are used by military, or military backed, regimes to intimidate 'subversives' and to repress antigovernment sentiment. They also serve to keep the families, associates and friends of the disappeared in constant anguish and terror. To qualify as a 'subversive', victims may be prominent voices of opposition or 'intellectuals' or professionals who may command the respect of the local community. Commonly, however, the victims may have done little more than voice their opinion, attend a rally or belong to a group – such as a trade union – deemed to be opposing the government. The hoped for result is to stifle all political and social activity within the society leaving the established government to rule with impunity.

A 'disappearance' begins with the kidnapping of an individual, or a whole family, and taking them to an undisclosed location. They are then interrogated (whether they have any information or not), tortured, and eventually, and most likely, killed. A few victims are released after torture, primarily to let each tell their story and aid the spreading of rumour and fear in the community.

The second phase is the denial that the person or family were ever taken. The reign of terror falls then, not on the initial victim, but on the people that look for them. They find themselves confronting a faceless bureaucracy and an aggressive police force which depicts them as 'trouble makers' or subversives. In many cases, simply for asking questions, the family and friends find that they are facing arrest, torture and possible 'disappearance' themselves.

Perhaps the most sinister element in cases of disappearance is this simple denial that anything has happened at all. Those remaining are left only with their memories of the vanished. Without knowing the truth about what has happened, they face a future where they cannot recollect their relative or friend without reawakening a flicker of hope that they might one day return. It has been described as like living with a ghost – they are not dead and yet they are not living. The family becomes effectively trapped in time, they cannot move on.

In 1983 in Argentina, a group called 'The Mothers of Plaza de Mayo' was formed after the removal of the military regime in order to bring pressure to trace their loved ones. They often used the symbol of an outline of a body painted on walls and pavements to represent the image of the 'disappeared' – the 'space that defines their absence'. Even years after the creation of an elected government, the discovery of mass graves and the identification of some of the missing, the victims are still referred to as 'the disappeared' and not as 'the dead'.

The dance at the end of A Mother's Voice is inspired by groups of women in Chile who gather in town squares across the country to protest and publicise the 'disappearance' of their husbands, children and relatives. They dance the Gueca (or Cueca) – a traditional Chilean courting dance. They perform the Gueca 'Solo' in that they dance alone yet many wear photographs of their loved ones pinned to their clothes. Whilst repressive governments may ban rallies or protest marches, few would ban people from – as the women who perform the dance would say – simply dancing.

Although the emphasis in A Mother's Voice is on the subject of 'disappearance' this abuse of human rights is seldom the only such abuse committed. The use of torture subsequent to the kidnapping sometimes at infamous centres of confinement such as the Villa Grimaldi is largely a matter of course. It would not be appropriate to discuss the nature of such torture used here but it is an important – if disturbing – area of research. Sadly the findings will show that whilst we often confine torture and torture chambers to the medieval past, very little has changed – the methods used have simply become more 'sophisticated'.

Much use is often made of 'Citizen's militias' to facilitate the kidnapping. These are often little more than criminal gangs sanctioned by the government or police force who turn a blind eye to their criminal activities in return for their support in the suppression of the society. These are the faceless 'shadows' in *A Mother's Voice* – the murderers, gangsters and torturers who occupy a place outside of regular society, supported but never acknowledged by the government. Murder and the use of so called 'death squads' is often rife with witnesses usually reluctant to come forward, knowing that to do so is to invite tragedy into their own lives.

RESOURCES

Finding more information about disappearances and human rights abuses is an important part of the preparation for a performance of 'A Mother's Voice'. Fortunately there is a good supply of active sources for this.

The Internet

The Internet is an excellent source, particularly as many of the organisations concerned with human rights abuses use the web as a primary means of campaigning and distributing information. Many of these sites will contain details of torture and other human rights abuses which you might find disturbing.

An obvious choice here is the web site of Amnesty International (www.amnesty.org). This well known organisation takes a non-political stance and campaigns against human rights abuses all over the world. Their web site contains a proliferation of background reports, news stories, campaign details and links to many other sources. Through the organisation you can also obtain written and video materials to help support your research.

Another organisation that is very useful is Human Rights Watch (www.hrw.org) which has a similar remit to Amnesty International. Its web site again has a wealth of helpful information and details of ongoing campaigns.

The Vanished Gallery (www.yendor.com/vanished) is an emotive site (some of which is in Spanish) which primarily focuses on the missing in Argentina. The site contains a good deal of useful information including accounts of disappearances and personal testimony and appeals from relatives of the missing. Particularly moving is the Wall of Memory which contains thousands of images and background profiles of vanished persons.

The following sites are also valuable sources:

www.desaparecidos.org/eng.html

www.derechos.org

www.derechoschile.com

www.madres.org (Official site of The Mothers of Plaza de Mayo)

The above sites all have significant English language content but some parts are in Spanish. If you have a good understanding of Spanish then a search of the Internet will lead to many other interesting and informative sources.

Other Resources

An obvious point of reference here is the work of Ariel Dorfman whose plays, *Death and the Maiden* and *The Widows* both deal with similar issues. He has also written widely on his experiences of human rights abuses and his poetry can be a source of inspiration. There is a film version of *Death and the Maiden* available.

The film *Missing* (1982) concerns the search by an American father – played by Jack Lemmon – for his son who has 'disappeared' during the military coup in Chile. In some ways the character played by Lemmon in the movie undergoes a transformation that is similar to that of Constantia in that his naive assumptions are stripped away as he is forced to face the truth.

Many well known popular musicians have been inspired and touched by the plight of the women. Artists like Sting and U2 in songs such as 'They Dance Alone' (Sting) and 'Mothers of the Disappeared' (U2) have shown their own commitment to publicise and support those who have their human rights abused.

The choreographer, Christopher Bruce, developed his dance 'Ghost Dances' in response to the situation in South America. This is a tremendously moving and evocative piece which can be inspirational to a cast performing the play. There are many echoes of the ominous presence and movements of the Ghosts used in 'Ghost Dances' in the Ghosts in A Mother's Voice. The dance also captures the resilience and strength of the people in spite of their dreadful situation.

Music

There is a call for a great deal of music in A Mother's Voice. Your actual choice of music will largely depend on exactly where you choose to set the piece. In the original production the music used had a particularly 'Andean' flavour. The evocative and haunting combination of flutes, guitars and pan pipes proved to be particularly powerful. We frequently used music to underscore parts of the action.

The ideal would be to have a live group of musicians as part of the presentation, however unless you are extremely fortunate in this respect, you will probably have to rely on recorded music. There is a good deal of pan pipe music available and you should exercise a little caution here – much of this is not remotely genuine with synthesizers replacing the pan pipes. Do try to obtain authentic music wherever possible. As Ernesto says 'The spirit of the people is in the dance' – it is unlikely to be so evident in the technological pulse of the synthesizer.

The music that accompanies 'Ghost Dances' is particularly appropriate and is available on CD performed by the group 'Incantation'. Although European musicians, Incantation use genuine instruments and perform both traditional songs and their own interpretations of South American and world music. Other albums by the band include *Panpipes of the Andes* and *Incantation* both of which contain very effective pieces.

There are of course many genuine South American musicians and bands such as Rumillajta whose music is increasingly available in this country through labels such as Tumi. With many internet music resellers now acting on an international basis it is possible to access an extremely wide range of suitable music with comparative ease.

Remember that formal permission must be obtained for the use of all recorded music which is used in performances.

AN AUTHOR'S NOTE

Rehearsing and performing *A Mother's Voice* can be a powerful and moving experience. Particularly when working with young people it can also be something of a journey – just as it is for Constantia – from innocence to experience. If you undertake effective research for the production then you will uncover a great deal of – at times – shocking information about the capacity for man's inhumanity to his fellow man. Whilst this is clearly present in *A Mother's Voice* I do not see it as a pessimistic piece but rather a celebration of the resilience of the human spirit. In spite of everything, the people still hold their heads up, still maintain their resolution and they still dance.

It is worth reminding yourself whilst rehearsing that real people somewhere in the world are actually suffering the actual pain, suffering and indignity that you are fortunate enough to only be portraying on stage. A bucket collection for a charity such as Amnesty International at the end of each show may not change the world but it may help to change it a little.